From Mother
to Daughter

From Mother to Daughter

From Mother to Daughter

Advice and Lessons for a Good Life

Sherry Conway Appel

ST. MARTIN'S PRESS   NEW YORK

Design by Sara Stemen

LIBRARY OF CONGRESS CATALOGING-IN-PUBLICATION DATA

Appel, Sherry Conway.
From mother to daughter: advice and lessons for a good
life/Sherry Conway Appel.
p.   cm.
ISBN 0-312-13498-3
1. Women—Quotations, maxims, etc.   2. Quotations,
English.
I. Title.
PN6084.W6A66   1995
081—dc20
95-33986
CIP

10 9 8 7

Books are available in quantity for promotional or
premium use. Write to Director of Special Sales,
St. Martin's Press, 175 Fifth Avenue, New York,
N.Y. 10010, for information on discounts and terms,
or call toll-free (800) 221-7945. In New York, call
(212) 674-5151 (ext. 645).

In loving memory of my mother,
Helen Leona Keyzer Conway,
and for my sweet daughter,
Leah Helen Appel

Introduction

A few weeks after my daughter was born, I was pacing the floors at 2 A.M., trying to bring some comfort to my colicky baby. Walking by our large patio doors, I glanced outside. In the dim light my reflection in the glass made it appear as if there were three or four of me, receding back into the night. My mother had died the year before, and with her had gone any words of advice about caring for a newborn. Yet in this strange reflection it seemed as if she were standing there with me, with her mother looking over her shoulder, stretching on into infinity, mom after mom, watching over me. In that moment I understood that she was there, and always would be. Her spirit, her warmth, and her loving ways would guide me as I cared for my child. I was not alone in my motherhood.

Now my little girl is eleven and she has a

seven-year-old brother, and time and time again I hear my own mother's words of advice and love in the things I say to them. "Don't run with a popsicle stick in your mouth." "Remember to make your bed before you leave your room in the morning." And, of course, "You are the most wonderful daughter and son in the whole world."

I wish my mother could have lived to see my children. I would have loved to share with her my "mothering" discoveries. Now I understand the reasons behind her anxieties about us, especially one which really drove us crazy. When we were growing up, to our annoyance, she always had to know where we were—which friends, which store, which movie theater. And, later, when we were old enough to travel, we always had to call and let her know we had arrived safely. By the time we were out of college, this behavior seemed ridiculous. But now that I am a mother, I understand completely. It doesn't seem a bit strange. I would like her to know this, and to know that I ask the same of my children, and probably will continue to do so until they are grown up and have children of their own. They are extensions of me, and just as I have to know where my hands and feet are, I have to know where my children are. They are part of me.

Mothers and daughters have always had interesting relationships. My mother was thirty-nine when she had me, which was unusual in those times. I was her fourth child, and she had run through a lot of childrearing by the time I came along. My brother (who was born three years later) and I provided her with many challenges. But there was one constant that never changed. Through all the admonitions and all the advice, in fact probably *because* of the admonitions and the advice, all of us knew that we were loved, and loved deeply. It was the best lesson she ever taught us.

—*Sherry Conway Appel*

Life

Mother knows best.

When in doubt, ask your momma.

Trust yourself.

$\mathcal{A}$lways treat people as if they may someday be on your jury.

Remember that you are known by the company you keep; so always surround yourself with people of good character.

There is absolutely nothing you can't do. (But you may have to give up something else to do it.)

$\mathcal{M}$y mother taught me the importance of devotion to family. She taught me to believe that I could do anything I put my mind to. When her friends asked, "Lillian, did you teach Lee to cook?" She would reply, "Hell no, I taught her to read."

She lived her life in such a way that I knew clearly what was valuable and what was not. While bedridden—unable to read or walk—she would say, "Honey, growing old ain't for sissies."

—*Lee Lacy*

Plan ahead.

Try to think of all sides of a question. Intelligence without understanding is jade without the carving—just a rock.

If you don't like the results, change the game. If you can't be Miss Universe, try to be the best-looking nuclear physicist—it's all the category you choose to compete in.

$\mathcal{F}$ailure is not falling down,
failure is not getting up.

Don't fall before you're pushed.

If you tried, you didn't fail.

When you fall, pick up something
while you're down there.

The essentials first: skills to survive—
then worry about meaning and pleasure.

Stick to your guns.

Don't get so big you forget where you come from.

You pass this way but once.
Any good you can do, do it now.

If you don't think well of yourself,
no one will think anything of you.

My mother was a gem. She always told us not to be quitters. In seventh grade our school was holding cheerleading tryouts, so a friend and I practiced and practiced. The morning of the tryouts, my friend called to say that she thought we didn't have a chance, so she was not going to try. My mother said, "If you don't try out you will never know." I did our routine solo and made cheerleader. Her encouragement meant the difference.
—*Susan Conway Himes*

$\mathcal{D}$on't say no very often,
but when you do, mean it.

Be tolerant. Everyone has talent.
Everyone is different.

If you believe something is impossible, it will be.

Don't complain that there's no wind.
Get out the oars and row.

When we were asked to do something that we didn't want to, we said, "Wait." She would say, "Weight's what broke the wagon down."
—*Carol Deal*

If something needs to be done,
do it as soon as you notice it.

If you are always getting ready to do something,
it will never get done.

It's a long road that never has any turns in it.

Nothing is taken from you that you cannot learn to live without. (This was Mom's comment when we broke or lost something.)

If you need the rain, you've got to put up with all the thunder and lightning that comes with it.

Don't forget that you're in charge of your life.
If you have a problem, deal with it right away.
Never hide from your problems, they won't
disappear all by themselves.

Be yourself (once you figure out who you are).

A smile and a thank-you won't cost you a dime.
But not doing either may cost you later.

$\mathcal{M}$y mother, Ho Po-Lan, taught by telling anecdotes and stories that tied us to our Chinese heritage. The message was that to be Chinese, female, and intelligent was often painful. Despite this, all my mother's women friends seemed to have titanium cores. There was always laughter overlaying their sadness.

—*Terry Jones*

Be brave. Timid people never
amount to very much.

$\mathcal{I}$t's just as bad to doubt everything
as it is to believe it.

Be careful what you ask for, you may get it.

Be your own woman. Don't waste your time
comparing yourself to others.

Be with, be for—but not against.

Always carry a book.

Don't believe everything you read
in the newspaper.

$\mathcal{D}$on't ask other people to do things for you that you can do for yourself.

If you don't ask, you're never going to learn.

The first hundred years and the first million dollars are the hardest.

If you want people to think you're smart,
learn to listen.

Don't listen to other people's secrets. They always
expect you to tell them yours in return.

Learn to do things for yourself (sew on a button,
change the oil) but always appreciate someone's
offer to do it for you.

$\mathcal{P}$roblems always look smaller after a warm meal and a good night's sleep.

Slow down, don't be in such a hurry. It doesn't do any good to run if you're headed down the wrong road.

Don't spend time worrying about things you can do nothing about.

Make up your mind. If you try to sit between two seats you're going to end up on the ground.

One good way to end up looking foolish is to pretend you know something you don't.

First impressions go a long way
and last a long time.

If you don't make mistakes,
you don't make anything.

Shoot for the moon.

Never use the truth to hurt someone.

Don't say that something isn't good, say you don't like it or it just doesn't work for you. There's an important difference.

Just because you own a rosary doesn't make you a nun.

$\mathcal{I}$f you're going to have trouble, better to
have it at the beginning than at the end.

Wait until nightfall before saying
it's been a good day.

If you want something more than anything,
be prepared to stake everything.

*I*f you learn things when you're young,
you'll remember them when you're old.

I remember my Aunty Gwen teaching me how to take eggs from under a sitting hen. I used to undertake the task with trepidation since the hens would always peck me to bits. The lesson, basically, consisted of setting your sights on where you thought the eggs would be, taking a deep breath and shoving your hand quickly and firmly under the hen. Finding that I could do this—after a bit of practice—without any painful retaliation, made me very proud of myself. And even today if I am faced with a prickly problem, I plan my attack, take a deep breath, and plunge forward to reach my goal.
—*Penny Cooper*

Don't think about the cost of doing something,
think about the cost of doing nothing.

No one was ever ruined by telling the truth.

If you're lonely or discouraged or unhappy,
do something for someone else.

*A*lways try to be a good sport.

If you're not good at one thing, keep trying.
You're bound to be good at something, even if
you haven't figured it out yet.

Finish what you start.

Keep your eye
on the ball.

$\mathcal{M}$y mother taught me that we are not in the world alone, that we are responsible for more than ourselves.

When we plant marigolds in the backyard, we are obligated to care for them, to water them, and to weed them so they have enough space and air and light to grow.

I learned that love entails obligation, that respect must be earned, and that "please" and "thank you" are not simply words to be mumbled at birthday parties.

My mother taught me to be a person.

—*Margot J. Fromer*

Every question doesn't necessarily deserve an answer. And some questions don't have any good answers.

Being a woman should never stop you from anything you want.

This too shall pass.

Your day will come.

Manners

$\mathcal{K}$eep your elbows off the table.

Save room for dinner.

Learn to use a finger bowl, just in case.

Don't have different sets of manners for different people. Treat everyone the same.

$\mathcal{G}$rowing up, the advice I *hated* most from my mother was, "See the other person's point of view—try to understand." I got this if someone was mean to me, hit me, or was just nasty in general.

A few days ago I called my daughter Carrie and asked her what advice of mine she remembers. She said she always hated being told always to try to see the other person's side of things.

I guess that proves what goes around comes around.

—*Sunday Wynkoop*

"Thank you" and "please" are the
keys to everyone's heart.

Always introduce a young person to an older
one, a man to a woman, and a boy to a girl.

If an older person gets on a crowded bus,
stand up and give her or him your seat.

Always write thank-you notes, but never
send store-bought sympathy cards.

Never say, "Remember me?" to a person.
If you have to ask, they usually don't.

Don't put your glass on a table unless
there's a coaster. Or use a napkin.

With dips, remember—only one dip per chip.

It's okay to sing for your supper, but once you sit down, there's no singing at the table.

Learn to tolerate others' differences; they're not different from you, you're different from them.

Children and Family

*T*reat your children like plants—with lots of sunshine and room to grow.

Read to your children every night and they'll be readers for life.

Eat with your children. It's the best way to learn what's going on in their lives.

Always see that your children have
something to look forward to.

Two children is a perfect number, but it would be
terribly hard to stop unless you had a daughter.

Try to make each child feel special. Whenever
a baby is born into a family, be sure to bring a
little gift for the other siblings.

When I was four, my mother wrote me this note:

My Dear,

Don't hurry so;
There's ample time.
Why must you rush?
At four, your little legs
can scarcely make the pace
you set for them.
Start now to temper life, while yet a child.
     —*Ruth Rice Crone*

Subscribe to *National Geographic* as soon as your child is old enough to hold a magazine.

Put baby oil on Band-Aids and let them sit for ten minutes. They come off without an "ouch."

Buy children's clothes big.

Be sure you count the Easter eggs before you hide them.

Write down the funny things your kids say as soon as they say them. Otherwise you'll forget.

Start exposing your kids to culture
(theater, elegant restaurants, New York City)
at a very young age.

Don't name your child something too unusual;
they'll probably get a nickname you'll hate.
But don't pick a name from the top ten either
or there'll be hard times in kindergarten.

"Try a little taste of everything." My mother was a trained dietitian so our diet was healthy. We had to eat at least one bite of everything. I still hate rutabaga but I learned to try everything. I still enjoy the tasting. . . .

—*Kit Kowalke*

When making peanut butter and jelly sandwiches, always put peanut butter on both sides of the bread and the jelly in the middle. That way the sandwich doesn't get soggy.

If you can't be there when your teenagers come home from school, keep the lights on, and leave a note and an interesting snack.

You're never too old to sit on your mother's lap.

Family comes first.

Never discuss family problems
with the neighbors.

Always stick up for your brothers and sisters.

No matter where you go or what you do, home
is always there for you to come back to.

One of the best Halloween costumes my mother ever made was turning my older brother into a tube of toothpaste when he was a small child. Today this seems almost prophetic since he ultimately chose dentistry as a profession!

—*Beth Della-Bella*

Children want limits: limits make them feel safe.

There is no greater love than that
of a mother for her child.

$\mathcal{I}$ learned from my daughter as much as my daughter learned from me. She was somewhere around eight when she planted both feet on the ground, crossed her arms, and told me that something I had done was not fair. To which I said that "the world is not fair." To which she promptly replied, "Well, you don't have to add to it."

She gave me pause with that thought.

—*Beverly R. Silverberg*

Having a daughter is a wonderful treasure; mothers and daughters can be best friends.

Health

$\mathcal{F}$or an upset stomach, ginger ale and saltine crackers in small doses are hard to beat.

As a child, my mother instilled in me a love of reading. In the eighth grade, I remember being home sick and reading *Exodus* by Leon Uris. She told me she was going to send a note to school saying I was home "sick in bed with Exodus."
—*Anne F. Ridgely*

Exercise every day. If you don't have time to work out, run the sweeper to the Rolling Stones.

Every once in awhile you may need to take a mental health day: call in sick to work, skip class, get a sitter for the kids, and take off—it doesn't matter whether you go to the beach or just drive around listening to your favorite radio station. The important thing is to get time to yourself.

$\mathcal{D}$rink a lot of water, it makes your skin glow and keeps you healthy.

If your doctor prescribes a medicine and you take it for two days and don't feel any better, it's probably the wrong medicine.

Change the batteries in your smoke detectors every January, whether they need it or not.

A woman can greatly reduce her incidence of heart attacks and strokes by eating carrots, spinach, and apricots.

$\mathcal{M}$y mother was more complex than I was. Any woman who would get a divorce during the Depression with two children to raise must have wanted it badly.

She had no hobbies or time for anything but work. She used to insist, "You are not to smoke." And of course I did.

—*Irene T. Appel*

Eat *all* your vegetables.

Always wear a big hat at the beach. It protects your skin and makes you feel very seductive.

Fashion and Clothing

*A*lways shop the sales rack first.

If you can afford only one good evening dress,
get it in black, and buy five pairs of really
stunning earrings to change the look.

When you get dressed up, put on everything
you want, just the way you want it. Then take
off one thing. (Preferably not the dress.)

My mother was one of nine daughters born to Polish immigrants. She married young and lost her husband at a very young age. She raised three daughters on her own. The most descriptive word I can think of to describe her is "generous." Just retired, she recently complained that she was having trouble finding six-inch red heels for dancing the polka.

—*Patricia Meronoff*

Patent leather shoes go with anything.

Your shoes should match your purse.

When you get home at night always change
your shoes. It will give you extra energy
and make the shoes last longer.

Never wear the same pair of shoes
two days in a row.

$\mathcal{I}$f you ever find the perfect bra, buy six.

Make sure there's a cotton crotch.

If you put new pantyhose in the freezer for
a day or two, they don't run as easily.

$\mathcal{T}$he power of my mother's words became very obvious to me ten years ago when I was involved in a very serious car crash. As I lay in the car bleeding, with several broken limbs and in severe shock, my first conscious thought was, "My God, what underwear did I wear?"

The first EMS technician ran up, and, to see how badly I was injured, asked me what my name was.

I replied, "Underwear."

The poor man thought I was in a lot worse shape than I really was.

—*Pam Beer*

$\mathcal{M}$asking tape can work wonders
for an errant hem.

Always carry a comb, a needle and thread,
and safety pins in your purse.

Make sure you know what you
look like from the back.

When you pack a bag for a trip, put in
everything you want. Then take two
things out before you close it.

Wearing black always makes you look thinner.

Always buy comfortable clothes.
Don't just follow fashion.

Get the settings of your rings checked every year.

Cooking and Entertaining

*I*f you can read, you can cook.

All good cooks burn (or cut) themselves
every once in awhile.

Clean up as you cook.

Always flirt with your butcher.

*P*ass the salt and pepper at the same time.

Cold food always needs more
salt than warm food.

When using a microwave, add salt
and pepper after cooking.

$\mathcal{F}$or the last few years of her life, my mother was in poor health. At one point, she was unable to eat. In despair, her doctors sent her home, thinking perhaps that *my* cooking might appeal to her. My husband and I made our very best meals, but a few bites was all she could manage. Then one day, my mother got out of bed and prepared an enormous and delicious meal and ate quite a bit of it, too. We didn't do any more cooking for her.

—*Susan Darter Hunt*

When in doubt about what to do, bake a cake.

Never slam a door when you have a cake
or soufflé in the oven, as it may fall.

Knead your biscuits with a light hand
or you'll have stones for dinner.

Never roll out a pie crust more than once.
If you do, it will be as tough as nails.

Don't wash mushrooms before you put them in the refrigerator. And store them in paper bags.

Always start bacon in a cold pan.

When making applesauce, use as many different types of apples as possible.

When cooking with tomatoes, always add a pinch of sugar.

$\mathcal{I}$f you want to have a successful party, plan the food and decorations around a theme and play great music—loud.

At parties, shake hands and mingle. Remember, guests have a responsibility to make a party work.

When giving a dinner party, always serve mashed potatoes but never corn on the cob, and something chocolate for dessert. Go to the living room for coffee.

Choose between having two drinks before dinner or wine with the meal. If you have both you probably will regret it the next day.

If your house looks reasonably neat, it doesn't have to be spotless. If company comes, turn off as many lights as possible and use a lot of candles.

Food should look as beautiful as possible when you serve it. Every day.

Home

$\mathcal{P}$lants die—buy new ones.

Big plants are easier to care for than small ones.

Water your overhead hanging plants by
putting a few ice cubes in the pot.

Always set a time for dinner.
Breakfast and lunch can be any time at all.

Never put a jar or a bottle
on the table at mealtime.

It is not a sign of weakness to use paper plates.

My mom always admonished me for worrying about cleaning my house and running the vacuum so much. Her final word on the subject was usually, "No one ever wanted to have 'She kept a clean house' on her tombstone."

—*Anne F. Ridgely*

Separate the lights and the darks.

Don't put your bras in the dryer.

Put a load of laundry in the washer when
you leave for work, move it to the dryer
when you come home.

Buy dark towels.

$\mathcal{M}$y mother bought an artificial Christmas tree and after a number of years setting the tree up and taking it down, she simply decided to put a large green plastic bag over it, and leave it in a corner of the family room. Then presto, the next Christmas (or any time, for that matter), she took the green plastic bag off and we were ready for our celebration! She said that this made Christmas easier, and that it allowed more time for other things.

—*Patty Craley*

Always put the tinsel on the Christmas
tree one piece at a time.

Clean up spilt milk very carefully or it will smell.

Always make your bed before leaving the house.

Hard work was her card dealt by life. She accepted it and made her house a home, sparkling clean, sunny, and wholesome.
> —*Peggy A. Cavender*

What makes a room beautiful is not furniture or flowers or paintings but light, and you can do a lot of that yourself by painting the whole place white. Off white. A very slightly warm white is best.

Put everything in its own place and you'll always know where everything is.

Put fabric softener sheets in your teenage son's sneakers to keep them from getting too ripe.

In sewing, it's the finishing that counts.
Always make a nice hem.

Keep a magnet in your sewing box
to help pick up dropped needles.

Cut your thread on an angle and
it will be easier to thread onto a needle.

It's no use saying, "Don't get a dog." But don't get a dog until your children are old enough to walk him.

Three or four months is a good age to get a puppy. But you don't need to get him from a kennel.

Money

Always take out a line of credit
before you need it.

Do with what you have;
don't borrow from anyone.

Never buy anything at full price.

Mom took care of the little things, like shopping, cooking, cleaning, laundry, and making sure my brother, father, and I had everything we needed. Before my father passed away, Mom had never written a check. Now she balances her checkbook, takes care of all the bills, runs the house, and takes the car for oil changes and maintenance. I admire her grit, her ability to pick up the pieces of her life, and her independence.

—*Beverly R. Silverberg*

Husbands and wives should pool their material belongings into "ours," rather than separating them into "mine." It makes for an easier and healthier relationship.

Never go grocery shopping when you're hungry.

Plain old petroleum jelly is just as
good as that expensive stuff.

Turn out the lights when you leave a room.
It sounds silly to a child but added up over
a year it can save you money.

$\mathcal{B}$uying cheap is always a waste of money.

Never skimp when you're buying leather goods; you'll never have to replace a good quality handbag and you'll end up saving in the long run.

When buying by mail-order, always keep a copy of your order form in case there is a problem.

Keeping Up Appearances

You don't have to be beautiful;
you just have to walk as if you were.

Stand up straight, shoulders back, chest out.

Remember that presentation counts—
in food, in your work, and in yourself.

*I*f your hair looks nice and your shoes look nice, whatever you're wearing will look nice, too.

Always check your makeup in a light different from where you applied it.

Put your feet together when you're having your picture taken.

Too many cocktails can dry out the skin.

Smoking gives you age lines.

$\mathcal{A}$lways carry a handkerchief or a pack of tissues.

Learn to dance.

My grandmother was a constant source of spunk and wit. Even after suffering a major heart attack, she maintained her sense of humor. While I was visiting her in the hospital, her cardiologist commented on our resemblance. Grandma pointed out (much to this fourteen-year-old's embarrassment) I even had her bowlegs. "However," Grandma continued, "we'd rather call them 'Pleasure Bent.' "
—*Nancy Fissel Hauser*

Comb your eyebrows.

Brush your tongue.

When you really feel down, buy the reddest lipstick you can find.

Friendship

*A*in't nobody your best friend
like your momma.

"Remember well and bear in mind, a trusty friend
is hard to find." Inscription in a charm bracelet, a
gift to my mother from her sister.
                    —*Peggy A. Cavender*

$\mathcal{R}$emember to have fun, just not at someone else's expense.

Don't do things for people just because you feel sorry for them.

My mother was wise in many ways. When I was very little, she heard me playing "church" in my room. Apparently, God was in the class and misbehaving, whereupon I told God to "sit down and shut up." Her first thought was to tell me not to talk to God in that way, and then she thought it was better that I had such a close and friendly relationship with the deity.

—*Pam Beer*

When you go to the hospital to have your baby, don't have your best friend take care of your husband while you're gone.

When a friend breaks up with her boyfriend, never say anything bad about him. She may fall in love with him again.

Never be the one to give a friend bad news about a husband or boyfriend. Someone else, usually an enemy, will always do that job.

$\mathcal{N}$ever room with a close friend. It's the best way to destroy a friendship.

A sure way to lose a friend is to loan her money or clothing you really care about.

When my roommate had worn me out with her romantic woes, I finally bet her that she wouldn't think about *him* if she starved herself. I was amazed. She lasted twenty-four hours before deciding that her only thought was for a grilled cheese.

—Terry Jones

Love, Men, Relationships

$\mathcal{D}$on't do anything at night that you'll
feel bad about in the morning.

Just because a man can speak French
doesn't make him a gentleman.

Don't marry a man you think
you're going to change.

$\mathcal{B}$efore marriage keep your eyes wide open.
After marriage keep them half shut.

Relationships aren't fifty-fifty. If you expect
one hundred percent of someone's love, you
must give one hundred percent of yourself.

Take half the credit and half the blame
for any misunderstanding.

You can marry more money in a minute
than you can make in a lifetime.

It doesn't matter whether you marry a rich man
or a poor man: money comes and goes. It's
intelligence and ambition that stick around.

$\mathcal{D}$on't go fishing in a man's belongings because you just might find what you were looking for.

If you can take a beau away from another woman, then someone else will be able to take him away from you.

Don't blame the ocean because you haven't caught any fish.

If you're always depending on men, you're always going to be disappointed.

$\mathcal{F}$ind a man who is crazy about you and make him your best friend. I did! I consider myself the luckiest woman alive to be married to my husband.
—*Mary Hendley*

Always look good for your husband.

Love is very important, but your husband also likes you because you can make him laugh.

If you're running late, set the table and start cooking an onion. When your husband gets home, he'll think you've been cooking all day.

How a man treats his mother is a clear
indication of how he treats his wife.

Never marry a man who is still
living with his mother.

If you don't get married and have children,
who will take care of you when you get old?

You don't have to get married.

Be trusting and find something good in everyone, but always take a long hat pin and mad money on a date.

Don't think that your love will change a man. Most people can't change and don't want to anyway.

After you get married, don't iron the first shirt. Let him do it himself.

Never trust a man who wears
a three-piece suit.

The best men walk on their toes.

Never go out with a guy whose belt
buckle is bigger than his head.

Weddings

$\mathcal{N}$ever get a wedding present monogrammed until after the wedding.

Ask someone to keep track of all the wedding presents, cards, etc. Otherwise writing thank-you notes will be a nightmare.

Don't have a friend take the wedding pictures. Hire a professional.

$\mathcal{B}$lankets are good wedding presents. It may not seem very exciting to the bride and groom, but they'll remember you in the years to come every time they get the blanket out to make up the guest bed.

When you're in the middle of planning a wedding and everything seems impossible, just keep in mind that all you really need is the guy you're going to marry and a minister/rabbi/judge. The essentials are easy and the details are ultimately unimportant.

Remember: most weddings only take twenty minutes.

The morning of my wedding, Mother rather hesitantly shared with me a family tradition. She gave me fifty dollars in cash which I was to keep on hand so that "I could always come home." The airline fare from Washington, D.C., to Springfield, Illinois, was fifty dollars at that time. She explained that all the women in our family (presumably she herself and my sister) always relied on this insurance.

—*Ellen M. Bozman*

Work and Education

All my life I remember my mother and aunts telling about being awakened on Monday morning by their mother with, "Wake up, it's Monday. Tomorrow is Tuesday, then Wednesday, and the week is half gone already and we've got nothing done!"

—*Kathryn Herrod Letson*

Make decisions in the morning,
that's when your brain is at its sharpest.

Bessie Bowling Morse was born on February 2, 1903, and was raised in Nelson County, Virginia. She was the youngest of eight children. She worked as a maid and then as a companion for two of the richest white families in Nelson County most of her life. She was the first black woman to drive a Model T Ford.

—*Shirley Clark*

If you can read, you can do anything.

$\mathcal{U}$se your imagination.

Be flexible.

Take notes.

You always get your best ideas in the shower,
in the middle of the night, or driving to work.
Keep pen and paper handy to write them down
immediately! (You will *not* remember them later.)

If you're not the lead dog,
the scenery never changes.

If you're supposed to be the leader, make sure
what direction you're heading in before you start.

The advice that rings through my memory is, "Be a
leader, not a follower." Sometimes that was diffi-
cult to follow through on, but in the end it always
paid off. The highest tribute I could pay my
mother is that I am trying to be the woman I
believe she is.

—*Gail Pennybacker Rose*

$\mathcal{A}$ct as if you will always succeed.

If you ask people for the impossible,
you'll get the best possible.

Always act like the winner when you lose.

Just because the surface of the pond is
calm doesn't mean there aren't
crocodiles waiting underneath.

$\mathcal{M}$y mom often told me to "rise above it" when I was growing up. Little did my mother know that this simple saying would act as a seed in my life, sowing confidence, humility, and strength. Even today, I am often in situations in which I need to displace myself for a moment, reflect on "rising above it" and choose to act on this wisdom.

—*Amy O. Ryan*

If you're going to complain, always
complain to the person who can help you.

Divide any big job into a succession of small jobs.

Never start the next thing
before you finish the first thing.

If you can't be good at something,
at least be enthusiastic.

When you deal with the public,
treat everyone equally, rich or poor.

Never make important decisions when
you're angry. Whatever you do will almost
always be wrong. Calm down, then act.

*I*f you have a number of jobs you don't
want to do, do the one you don't want
to do the most first.

If you want to get a job done, ask a busy person.

A thing is only worth so much time.

$\mathcal{N}$ever quit a job before you have another job.

Be careful when making a change. You might be trading one set of problems for another, so be sure that you'll like the new problems better than the old ones.

Don't be afraid of your boss. Better to
ask twice than be wrong once.

If you're the boss, give people the bad news
on Monday, and they'll be too busy during
the week to brood on it. Give them the
good news on Friday, so they can have
the weekend to celebrate.

If you're going to ask for a raise, do it over lunch.

Never sign anything that you
haven't already read.

There's no point in worrying about your
hair if they've chopped off your head.

Be careful not to promise
anything that you can't deliver.

Decide what you want to be,
then do what you have to do to be it.

With regard to career and motherhood—you
can have it all, just maybe not at the same time.

$\mathcal{D}$on't split infinitives.

Any job, big or small, is worth
doing well or not at all.

Don't try to find opportunity—make it.

Girls can mow lawns, too!

Your mind can concentrate fully on only one thing at a time. Organize your desk to implement that one task. Remove all other distractions.

Pay attention to yourself for a week and see where and how you waste time. Then do something about it.

*D*on't tell people what you're not going to do or what you would have done.

Education is paramount. Marriage will always be there if you want it.

Luck is always nice, but it's hard work that usually gets you what you want, and you need to want it more than anything.

Be productive but live life and have a good time.

Do it now.

My mother is my best friend. Words could never even scratch the surface of my admiration for and devotion to her. She is courageous, adventurous, warm, loving, and beautiful. I know how much I have been blessed, and never let a day go by without thanking God for her.

—*Irene Calabrese*

Special Thanks

$\mathcal{W}$e would like to thank the following mothers, daughters, aunts, and grandmothers for their generous contributions to this book. Reading their stories of joy, pain, love, humor, and patience brought us a sincere appreciation for the job of mothering. Many said they enjoyed the opportunity to sit down and write about their moms, or simply spend time thinking about their past relationships. One woman added, "Thanks for this. It felt good." If readers would like to contribute to future books on mothers and advice, you can write to us in care of our terrific editor, Ensley Eikenburg, at St. Martin's Press, 175 Fifth Avenue, New York, N.Y. 10010.

Barbara Conway Abbruzzese, Helen Leona Keyzer Conway; Irene Trippett Appel, Emma Busch Mason; Deirdre Ruckman Appel, Anna Rae Ruckman; Mary Ann Barrows, Daisy L. Meyer; Bonnie Beck; Pam Beer, June F. Beer; Donna Greenfield Belser; Barbara Bode; Ellen M. Bozman; Kellis E. Bunner, Dorothy L. Legg, Dorothy E. Armer; Irene Calabrese, Grazia Calabrese; Elizabeth Force Carson, Patricia L. Force; Linda S. Wernick Cassell, Jeanne Ann Wernick; Peggy A. Cavender, Effie Violet Jordan Cavender; Hilary L. Chiz; Shirley Clark, Bessie Bowling Morse; Penny Cooper, Aunty Gwen Cooper; Caryn Coyle, Claire Norma Stacey Coyle; Patty Craley; Ruth Rice Crone, Thelma Ryle Rice; Ann Davidson, Violet Olson Gunderson; Carol Deal; Mary DelPopolo, Florence Marie Pesanti DelPopolo; Beth Della-Bella, Mary Lou Della-Bella, Phyllis J. Norton; Kathleen Dragan, Helen Toohey; Nancy Duggan; Linda Eads, Eloise Eads, Beaulah W. DeJarnette; Kathleen Ewing, JoAnne Ewing; Yvonne Snyder Farley, Malwina Snyder; Elizabeth Farrell; Jamie Fear; Jocelyn C. Ferguson, Madeline J. Clark, Nora Clark Davis; Sandy Appel Fisher; Darlene Foster; Barbara Frank, Esther Mindel Frank; Amanda

Fisher Fredrickson; Margot J. Fromer; Lisa Garrison; Julie Himes Gerig, Susan Conway Himes; Linda Gray; Karen Elliott Greisdorf, Mary White Elliott; Lynn Gumbowski; Tara Hamilton, Esther Ennis, Patricia King; Geraldine Vickers Harrison, Linnie Faber Vickers; Nancy Fissel Hauser, Mary Fissel, Louise Bensel; Carla Haner; Joy E. Held, Joy Opal Gunnoe Dick; Mary Hendley, Frances Rose Wilson; Charlotte Henline; Debbie Herr; Estelle Forshaw Himes; Susan Darter Hunt, Blanche Boykin Beauregard; Ellen Jaffe, Molly C. Jaffe; Martha Siegfried Johnson, Mary Myrtle Power Siegfried; Patricia A. Jones, Maureen Rose McCormick Jones; Terry Jones, Ho Po-Lan; Karen Kalish, Berta S. Kalish, Estelle W. Kalish; Jodi Jett Karr; Allison E. Kofoet, Judith M. Kofoet; Kit Kowalke; Lee Lacy, Lillian Lam Hitchcock; Robin Latham; Kathryn Herrod Letson, Arrie Etta Herrod; Penny Lewandowski; Denise Lloyd; Karyn T. Lynch; Grace Madole; Allison McCall, Ruth Berke, Lizzie Kobre; Eugenia (Jean) Kelly McCall, Bridget Gormley Kelly; Susan Clem McKenna,

Jane Clem; Bonni McKeown, Virginia-Lou Austin McKeown; Patricia Meronoff, Eleanor Meronoff; Wendy Miller; Jan Mitchell, Mary Ellen Phillips; Evelyn Schietinger Morris, Ruth Evelyn Brock Schietinger; Barbara Moum, Pat Moum; Gladys Peterson Nemecek; Suzanne Ruckman Nowell; Margaret Oppenheimer; Bobbie Seifer Paul, Anne Satterthwaite Seifer, Freda Schultz Seifer, Edith Margerum Satterthwaite; Gail Pennybacker Rose, Dee Pennybacker; Dorothy Conway Pinegar, Sarah Sevier Conway; Margie Polk; Rachel Power, Virginia Power; Carolyn Psai, Dorothy Keswick; Cina Radler, Harriet Radler; Emily Isberg Reardon, Sylvia Waldman Isberg (stage name Sue Bailey); Abigail R. Reynolds, Rachel Ann Reynolds, Talma P. Robertson; Anne F. Ridgely, Dorothy Vandegrift Fleming; Becky Rinehart, Helen Marie Rinehart; Jill Ellen Rosenthal, Joyce Karp Lindmark; Stella Katchan Wheeler; Amy O. Ryan, Connie Ryan; Judi Scioli, Rhoda Nisenholtz; Rebecca L. Sheppard, Margaret G. Sheppard; Trudy Shultz; Beverly R. Silverberg, Anne Gubenko Rabner,

Nina Silverberg; Jane Elizabeth Slagter, Edith Elinore McMahan; Elisabeth M. Smeda, Ione M. Hoekenga; Lucye J. Snyder, Lillie Ann Rider; Jean Steele; Ruthann R. Stone; Susan Alfandre Swain, Rose Glasser Alfandre; Patricia (Patsy) Ticer, Margaret (Peggy) Keyser Smith; Eileen Toumanoff, Louise Thoron MacVeagh; Alexandra Truitt, Anne Dean Truitt; Patricia Warren, Ida Warren; Alissa Watkins, Maxine Roberts, Margie Bray; Ann Williams White, Sarah Elizabeth Stinnie Williams; Judy Conway Wilgus, Anna Sevier Facey, Nora Brown, Tracy Wilgus Weins; Betty Wilson; Page Winstead, Helen T. Vietor, Marion L. Winstead; Lisa Woo, Rosalie Yee Quil Woo; Sunday Wynkoop, Susan Hammett, Viola Roberts, Carrie Evans Wynkoop